THE BIG PICTURE
LEADER GUIDE

JEVON CALDWELL-GROSS
NICOLE CALDWELL-GROSS

THE BIG PICTURE

SEEING GOD'S DREAM FOR YOUR LIFE

LEADER GUIDE

Abingdon Press / Nashville

THE BIG PICTURE
SEEING GOD'S DREAM FOR YOUR LIFE
LEADER GUIDE

978-1-7910-2597-7

MANUFACTURED IN THE UNITED STATES OF AMERICA

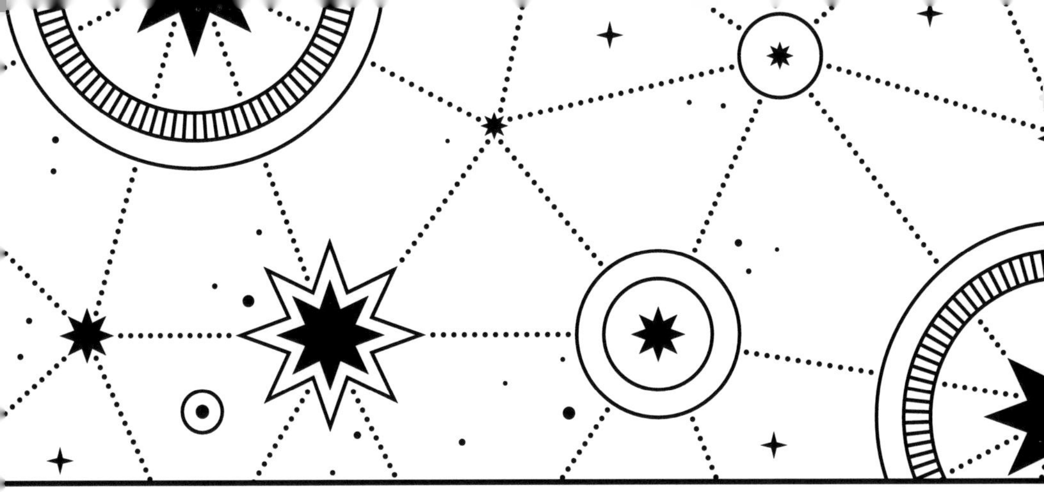

CONTENTS

To the Leader 7

1. I Can't See It 19

2. I'm a Survivor 28

3. Dreaming in Prison 37

4. Timing Is Everything 46

5. The Moment We've Been Waiting For 55

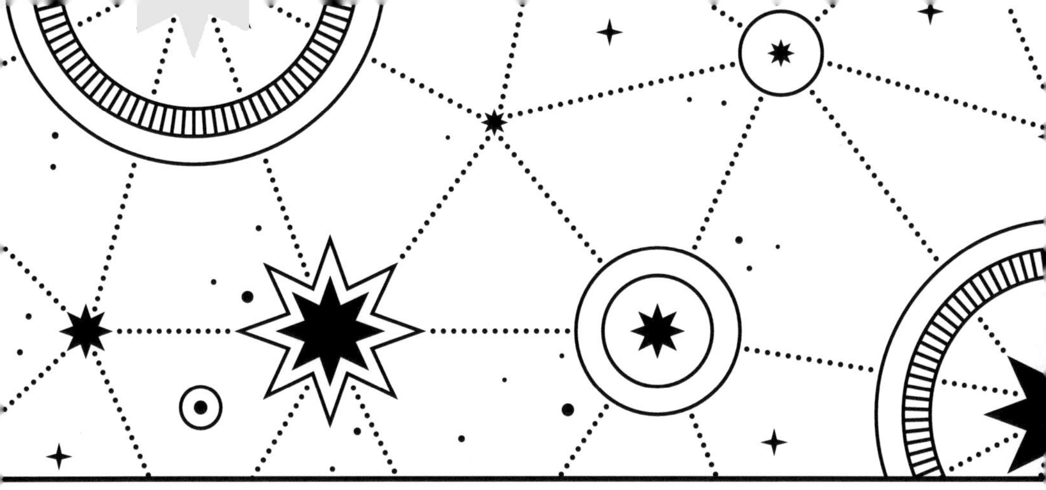

TO THE LEADER

In *The Big Picture: Seeing God's Dream for Your Life*, Jevon Caldwell-Gross and Nicole Caldwell-Gross invite you to see yourself as a dreamer, connecting the dots of God's grace and provision in your life, and recognize that God is at work in you and through you. By studying the story of Joseph in the Book of Genesis, you will learn to pay close attention to the story of your own life in a way that asks what God's dream is for you.

This Leader Guide is designed to help leaders of adult Christian small groups to discuss and learn from *The Big Picture* and apply its lessons to their lives. There are five sessions, corresponding to the five chapters of the book:

1. I Can't See It (Genesis 37:5-11)
2. I'm a Survivor (Genesis 37:19-28)
3. Dreaming in Prison (Genesis 40:1-8)
4. Timing Is Everything (Genesis 41:1, 8-12, 14-16)
5. The Moment We've Been Waiting For (Genesis 45:1-8)

How to Facilitate This Study

This study makes use of the following components:

- ***The Big Picture: Seeing God's Dream for Your Life***, by Jevon Caldwell-Gross and Nicole Caldwell-Gross.

- **This *Leader Guide***.
- ***The Big Picture DVD***, or access to the streaming video sessions via Amplify Media (www.amplifymedia.com).
- **The Bible**. A variety of translations is both allowable and desirable in your small group. Multiple translations allow you to compare wording and open the possibility for new insights into the text. Some great translations include the Common English Bible (CEB), New Revised Standard Version (NRSV), and New International Version (NIV).

Each session should take approximately 45–60 minutes to complete and consists of the following segments:

- **Session Goals**: Describes the objectives of this week's lesson.
- **Biblical Foundation**: Contains the key Scripture texts for this week's lesson.
- **Opening the Session**: Gather the group together, introduce the main ideas for this lesson with a brief discussion or activity, then open with prayer.
- **Watch the Video**: Watch the video session and discuss using the questions provided.
- **Discussion**: Discuss the Scripture passage and the relevant chapter of *The Big Picture* using the discussion questions that are provided in each section.
- **Closing**: Wrap up the session with a closing activity and end with prayer.

Helpful Hints

Preparing for Each Session

- Carefully read the corresponding chapter of *The Big Picture.*
- Prayerfully read the session's Biblical Foundation, noting questions and issues you need or want to study further. Consult trusted biblical references for more information.
- Gather Bibles for participants (and/or slides of the

session's Biblical Foundation for screen-sharing purposes), as well as paper or notebooks for people to write their responses when invited.

- Review the discussion questions for the session and select the ones you want to spend the most time with in your group. Be prepared, however, to adjust the session as group members interact and as questions arise. Prepare carefully, but allow space for the Holy Spirit to move in and through the group members and through you as facilitator.
- Prepare the space where the group will meet so that the space will enhance the learning process. Ideally, group members should be seated around a table or in a circle so that all can see one another.

Shaping the Learning Environment

- Create a climate of openness, encouraging group members to participate as they feel comfortable.
- Remember that some people will jump right in with answers and comments, while others need time to process what is being discussed.
- If you notice that some group members seem never to be able to enter the conversation, ask them if they have thoughts to share. Give everyone a chance to talk, but keep the conversation moving. Moderate to prevent a few individuals from doing all the talking.
- Communicate the importance of group discussions and group exercises.
- If no one answers at first during discussions, do not be afraid of silence. Count silently to ten, then say something such as, "Would anyone like to go first?" If no one responds, venture an answer yourself and ask for comments.
- Model openness as you share with the group. Group members will follow your example. If you limit your sharing to a surface level, others will follow suit.

- Encourage multiple answers or responses before moving on to the next question.
- Ask "Why?" or "Why do you believe that?" or "Can you say more about that?" to help continue a discussion and give it greater depth.
- Affirm others' responses with comments such as "Great" or "Thanks" or "Good insight"—especially if it's the first time someone has spoken during the group session.
- Monitor your own contributions. If you are doing most of the talking, back off so that you do not train the group to listen rather than speak up.
- Remember that you do not have to have all the answers. Your job is to keep the discussion going and encourage participation.

Managing the Session

- Honor the time schedule. If a session is running longer than expected, get consensus from the group before continuing beyond the agreed-upon ending time.
- Involve group members in various aspects of the group session, such as saying prayers or reading the Scripture.
- As always in discussions that may involve personal sharing, confidentiality is essential. Group members should never pass along stories that have been shared in the group. Remind the group members at each session: confidentiality is crucial to the success of this study.

Thank you for leading your group in this study of the *The Big Picture* by Jevon Caldwell-Gross and Nicole Caldwell-Gross. May your shared readings, discussions, and reflections enrich your faith and help you discover God's dream for your life.

Adapting for Virtual Small Group Sessions

Meeting online is a great option for a number of situations. During the time of a public-health hazard, such as the COVID-19 pandemic, online meetings are a welcome opportunity for people to converse while seeing one another's faces. Online meetings can also expand the "neighborhood" of possible group members, because people can log in from just about anywhere in the world. This also gives those who do not have access to transportation or who prefer not to travel at certain times of day the chance to participate.

The guidelines below will help you lead an effective and enriching group study using an online video conferencing platform such as Zoom, Webex, Google Meet, Microsoft Teams, or another virtual meeting platform of your choice.

Basic Features for Virtual Meetings

There are many choices for videoconferencing platforms. You may have personal experience and comfort using a particular service, or your church may have a subscription that will influence your choice. Whichever option you choose, it is recommended that you use a platform that supports the following features:

- **Synchronous video and audio**: Your participants can see and speak to one another live, in real time. Participants have the ability to turn their video off and on, and to mute and unmute their audio.
- **Chat**: Your participants can send text messages to the whole group or individuals from within the virtual meeting. Participants can put active hyperlinks (i.e., "clickable" internet addresses) into the chat for other participants' convenience.
- **Screen Sharing**: Participants can share the contents of their screen with other participants (the meeting host's permission may be required).
- **Video Sharing**: Participants (or the host) can share videos and computer audio via screen share, so that all participants can view the videos each week.
- **Breakout Rooms**: Meeting hosts can automatically or manually send participants into virtual smaller groups and can determine whether the rooms end automatically

after a set period of time. Hosts can communicate with all breakout rooms. *This feature is useful if your group is large, or if you wish to break into smaller teams of two or three for certain activities. If you have a smaller group, this feature may not be necessary.*

Check with your pastor or director of discipleship to see if your church has a preferred platform or an account with one or more of these platforms that you might use. In most instances, only the host will need to be signed in to the account; others can participate without being registered.

Zoom, Webex, Google Meet, and Microsoft Teams all offer free versions of their platform, which you can use if your church doesn't have an account. However, there may be some restrictions (for instance, Zoom's free version limits meetings to 45 minutes). Check each platform's website to be sure you are aware of any such restrictions before you sign up.

Once you have selected a platform, familiarize yourself with all of its features and controls so that you can facilitate virtual meetings comfortably. The platform's website will have lists of features and helpful tutorials; often third-party sites will have useful information or instructions as well.

There are additional features on many that help play your video more effectively. In Zoom, for example, as you click the "share screen" option and see the screen showing your different windows, check at the bottom of that window to choose "optimize for video clips" and "share audio." These ensure that your group hears the audio and that, when sharing a clip, the video resolution is compressed to fit the bandwidth that you have.

In addition to videoconferencing software, it is also advisable to have access to slide-creation software such as Microsoft PowerPoint or Google Slides. These can be used to prepare easy slides for screen-sharing to display discussion questions, quotes from the study book, or Scripture passages. If you don't have easy access to these, you can create a document and share it—but make sure the print size is easy to read.

Video Sharing

For a video-based study, it's important to be able to screen-share your videos so that all participants can view them in your study session. The good news is, whether you have the videos on DVD or streaming files, it is possible to play them in your session.

All of the videoconferencing platforms mentioned above support screen-sharing videos. Some have specific requirements for assuring that sound will play clearly in addition to the videos. Follow your videoconferencing platform instructions carefully, and test the video sharing in advance to be sure it works.

If you wish to screen-share a DVD video, you may need to use a different media player. Some media players will not allow you to share your screen when you play copyright-protected DVDs. VLC is a free media player that is safe and easy to use. To try this software, download at videolan.org/VLC.

What about copyright? DVDs like those you use for group study are meant to be used in a group setting in "real time." That is, whether you meet in person, online, or in a hybrid setting, Abingdon Press encourages use of your DVD or streaming video.

What is allowed: streaming an Abingdon DVD over Zoom, Teams, or similar platform during a small group session.

What is not allowed: posting video of a published DVD study to social media or YouTube for later viewing.

If you have any questions about permissions and copyright, email permissions@abingdonpress.com.

Amplify Media. The streaming subscription platform Amplify Media makes it easy to share streaming videos for groups. When your church has an Amplify subscription, your group members can sign on and have access to the video sessions. With access, they may watch the video on their own ahead of your group meeting, watch the streaming video during your group meeting, or view it again after the meeting. Thousands of videos are on amplifymedia.com, making it easy to watch anytime, anywhere, and on any device from phones and tablets to smart TVs and desktops.

Visit amplifymedia.com to learn more or call 1-800-672-1789, option 4, to hear about the current offers.

Communicating with Your Group

Clear communication with your small group before and throughout your study is crucial no matter how you meet, but it is doubly important if you are gathering virtually.

Advertising the Study. Be sure to advertise your virtual study on either your church's website or in its newsletter, or both, as well as any social media that your church uses. Request pastors or other worship leaders to announce it in worship services.

Registration. Encourage people to register for the online study so that you can know all participants and have a way to contact them. Ideally, you will collect an email address for each participant so that you can send them communications and links to your virtual meeting sessions. An event planning tool such as SignUpGenius makes this easy and gives you a database of participants and their email addresses.

Welcome Email. Before your first session, several days in advance, send an email to everyone who has registered for the study, welcoming them to the group, reminding them of the date and time of your first meeting, and including a link to join the virtual meeting. It's also a good idea to include one or two discussion questions to "prime the pump" for reflection and conversation when you gather.

If you have members without internet service, or if they are uncomfortable using a computer and videoconferencing software, let them know they may telephone into the meeting. Provide them the number and let them know that there is usually a unique phone number for each meeting.

Weekly Emails. Send a new email two or three days before each week's session, again including the link to join your virtual meeting and one or two discussion questions to set the stage for discussion. Feel free to use any of the questions in the Leader Guide for this purpose. If you find a particular quote from the book that is especially meaningful, include this as well.

Facebook. Consider creating a private Facebook group for your small group, where you can hold discussion and invite reflection between your weekly meetings. Each week, post one or two quotes from the study book along with a short question for reflection, and invite people to respond in the comments. These questions can come straight from the Leader Guide, and you can revisit the Facebook conversation during your virtual meeting.

You might also consider posting these quotes and questions on your church's main Facebook page, inviting people in your congregation to join the conversation beyond your small group. This can be a great way to involve others in your study, or to let people know about it and invite them to join your next virtual meeting.

During Your Virtual Sessions

During your virtual sessions, follow these tips to be sure you are prepared and that everything runs as smoothly as possible.

Getting Ready

- Familiarize yourself with the controls and features of your videoconferencing platform, using instructions or tutorials available via the platform's website or third-party sites.
- Be sure you are leading the session from a well-lit place in front of a background free from excessive distractions.
- As leader, log into the virtual meeting early. You want to be a good host who is present to welcome participants by name as they arrive. This also gives you time to check how you appear on camera, so that you can make any last-minute adjustments to your lighting and background if needed.

Creating Community Online

- During each session, pay attention to who is speaking and who is not. Because of video and audio lags as well as internet connections of varying quality, some participants may inadvertently speak over one another without realizing they are doing so. As needed, directly prompt specific people to speak if they wish (for example, "Alan, it looked like you were about to say something when Sarah was speaking").

- If your group is especially large, you may want to agree with members on a procedure for being recognized to speak (for example, participants might "raise hands" digitally or type "call on me" in the chat feature).
- Instruct participants to keep their microphones muted during the meeting, so extraneous noise from their location does not interrupt the meeting. This includes chewing or yawning sounds, which can be embarrassing! When it is time for discussion, participants can unmute themselves.
- Remember some participants may wish to simply observe and listen—do not pressure anyone to speak who does not wish to.
- Always get your group's permission before recording your online sessions. While those who are unable to attend the meeting may appreciate the chance to view it later, respect the privacy of your participants.
- Communicate with your group in between sessions with weekly emails and Facebook posts to spark ongoing discussion.

In challenging times, modern technology has powerful potential to bring God's people together in new and nourishing ways. May such be your experience during this virtual study.

Help, Support, and Tutorials

The creators of the most popular virtual meeting platforms have excellent, free resources available online to help you get started using their platform, which teach you everything from how to join a meeting as a participant to how to use the more advanced features like video sharing and breakout rooms. Most of them offer clear written instructions as well as video tutorials and also provide a way to contact the company in case you need additional assistance.

Below are links for five platforms: Zoom, Microsoft Teams, Webex, Google Meet, and GoTo Meeting. If you are using a different platform, go to their website and look for the "Help" or "Resources" page.

- **Zoom Help Center**: https://support.zoom.us/hc/en-us
  This help contains a comprehensive collection of resources to help you use the Zoom platform, including quick start guides, video tutorials, articles, and specific sets of instructions on various topics or issues you may run into.
- **Microsoft Teams Help & Learning**: https://support.microsoft.com/en-us/teams
  A collection of articles, videos, and instructions on how to use the Microsoft Teams platform. Teams offers a number of features. You are most likely to find the help you need for group meetings by navigating to the "Meetings" page, or by clicking "Microsoft Teams training" under "Explore Microsoft Teams."
- **Webex Help Center**: https://help.webex.com/en-us/
  This contains articles, videos, and other resources to help you use the Webex platform, with everything from joining the meeting to screen-sharing and using a virtual whiteboard.
- **Google Meet Help**: https://support.google.com/meet/
  This contains a list of support topics to help you use the Google Meet platform, in an easy-to-read expandable list that makes it easy to find just what you need.
- **GoToMeeting Support**: https://support.goto.com/meeting
  Here you'll find links with instructions on various topics to help you use the GoToMeeting platform.

General How-To

In addition to these official support pages, there are numerous independent sites online with great, clear instructions on using multiple platforms. Here is one excellent resource:

- **Nerds Chalk**: https://nerdschalk.com/
  This site is easily searchable and contains numerous articles and how-go guides, with clear titles to help you find exactly what you need. Simply search for either your chosen platform or what you are trying to accomplish—such as "breakout rooms" or "Zoom screen share"—and navigate to the most relevant link.

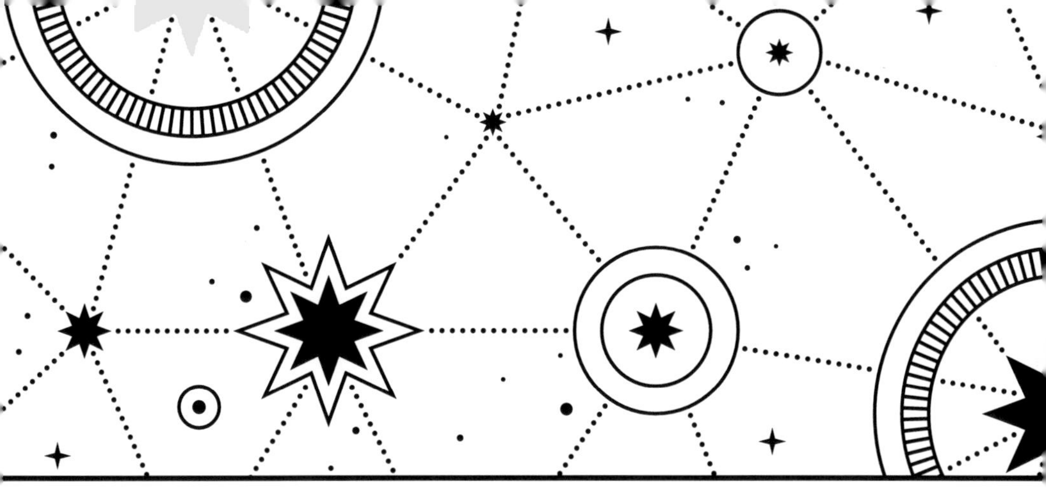

SESSION 1
I CAN'T SEE IT

Session Goals

In this opening session, participants (dreamers) will:

- begin to see themselves as dreamers with an active role in God's big picture for their lives,
- be oriented to the biblical story of Joseph and the spiritual lessons his narrative offers us as dreamers of God's big picture today,
- acknowledge the presence of ambiguity as we interpret God's dreams for ourselves, and
- examine the practical ways to respond when our dreams are met with doubt.

Biblical Foundation: *Genesis 37:1-11*

Jacob lived in the land of Canaan where his father was an immigrant. This is the account of Jacob's descendants. Joseph was

17 years old and tended the flock with his brothers. While he was helping the sons of Bilhah and Zilpah, his father's wives, Joseph told their father unflattering things about them. Now Israel loved Joseph more than any of his other sons because he was born when Jacob was old. Jacob had made for him a long robe. When his brothers saw that their father loved him more than any of his brothers, they hated him and couldn't even talk nicely to him.

Joseph had a dream and told it to his brothers, which made them hate him even more. He said to them, "Listen to this dream I had. When we were binding stalks of grain in the field, my stalk got up and stood upright, while your stalks gathered around it and bowed down to my stalk."

His brothers said to him, "Will you really be our king and rule over us?" So they hated him even more because of the dreams he told them.

Then Joseph had another dream and described it to his brothers: "I've just dreamed again, and this time the sun and the moon and eleven stars were bowing down to me."

When he described it to his father and brothers, his father scolded him and said to him, "What kind of dreams have you dreamed? Am I and your mother and your brothers supposed to come and bow down to the ground in front of you?" His brothers were jealous of him, but his father took careful note of the matter.

Preparation

As a leader of the study, you are embarking on a holy journey that could influence the faith life of every person in your group and every person with whom they connect. Make space and time to connect with God before you begin your session. Lift up the names of those who will join you, and ask for the presence of the Holy Spirit as you begin this journey.

You may consider lifting up this paraphrase of the prayer attributed to St. Patrick:

> Christ with me,
> Christ before me,

Christ behind me,
Christ in me,
Christ beneath me,
Christ above me,
Christ on my right,
Christ on my left,
Christ when I lie down,
Christ when I sit down,
Christ when I arise,
Christ in the heart of every person who is here today,
Christ in the mouth of everyone who shares today,
Christ in every ear that hears today.

Note that throughout this guide, and hopefully throughout your conversations, you will refer to each person as a "dreamer" and not as a participant. This language is intentional as we hope that throughout the study people will begin to see themselves as dreamers. They will begin to claim an identity as someone who has vision, influence, and direction over their life. This will seem awkward at first, but it is a powerful reminder for you and for those who share this journey. If we are all dreamers, then it implies the main idea of our work together: God has a big picture for each of our lives, and we are invited to dream with God in making it a reality.

Finally, prior to the session, invite each dreamer to bring a notebook. This notebook will be referred to as their dream book throughout each session. They are invited to reflect, discern, or write prayers in their dream books. This tool will be referred to throughout the sessions and is a way to engage people who may communicate best through writing. Additionally, long after the study this dream book may serve as a salient reminder of the spiritual lessons they gleaned during this journey.

Opening the Session

- Welcome everyone as they arrive. Take a moment to express your gratitude for their participation. Remind them that this is both a collective and an individual journey of discovering and rediscovering the presence of God in their lives. Remember that everyone is here by choice. Honor their decision to give a portion of their time to this group and to this study.

- Inform the group that over the next five weeks, the word *dreamer* will often be used to replace words like *participant* or *group member*. This will serve as a verbal and spiritual reminder of God's possibilities.
- Take a moment to familiarize yourself with the narrative surrounding Joseph's family. While this session starts at Genesis 37, it will be helpful to have a firm grasp on the family dynamics.
    - ◊ Invite the group of dreamers to recount the whole story of Joseph across Genesis 37–50.
      A study Bible may be useful to help you recall the main points of the story.
    - ◊ Invite a dreamer to read Genesis 37:1-11 aloud.
- As an opening activity, have each member recite this phrase:
    - ◊ I am a ____________ and I am a dreamer.
    - ◊ Each dreamer will fill in the blank with a piece of relevant information that best describes them (for example, I am a parent of three small children, and I am a dreamer. Or, I am recently retired, and I am a dreamer).
    - ◊ Have each dreamer share why they chose that word or phrase.
- What did you notice about the various responses? What does this suggest about "dreamers"?

Opening Prayer

God, as we begin this journey, we ask that your presence be with us. We open ourselves to the discussions we'll have, the lessons they'll teach us, and to each other. Over these next five sessions, expand our imaginations so that we can see your bigger picture for each of our lives. Help us to find your presence in every season of our lives. Help us remember those places we may have overlooked. We come to this moment with an expectation that you will meet us where we are. In Christ's name we pray. Amen.

Watch the Video

Play video for Session 1 using your DVD player or stream with Amplify Media. Discuss the following:

- Invite the dreamers to share one or two main points that resonated with them from this session.
- What aspects of Joseph's story challenge you the most? Why?
- Invite the dreamers to share their dreams. These dreams can either be individual or communal. As dreamers share, encourage them to draw and label small dots on a page in their dream books to represent these dreams.

Scripture and Book Study

Use the questions and activities below to discuss each section of the book and the opening of the Joseph story, Genesis 37:1-11.

It Was All a Dream

- Joseph was an average person born into a regular family. He had a very common job and yet was met with a God-sized dream. Share the names of people each of you would consider a dreamer. These can be famous people or those you know personally. They can be alive or deceased. What matters is that you think of them as dreamers.
- What qualities do these dreamers possess? What similarities and differences do you notice as the list of dreamers is shared?
- The book states, "*Much of what God will do in your life, you won't see coming*. You will try your best to make sense of what's in front of you, but it will seem

confusing and disconnected in the moment." Do you agree with this statement? If so, give examples of how you have seen this in your own life. If not, why?

- In many ways, finding your God-given dream is a journey of "noticing." Are there areas in your life where you need to pay closer attention in looking for the presence of God?
- A major component of this chapter rests on an observation by Søren Kirkegaard that suggests life is lived forward, but understood backward. What lessons do you think Joseph is learning early in his journey? What lessons have you learned in hindsight? Why is it so difficult to comprehend these lessons in the moment?

Why We Can't See It

- Through his dreams, God showed Joseph that something different was possible. What impact will this have on his perspective? How will it change the way he views himself and his family? How might his perspective stay the same?
- Describe a time when your perspective on something or someone changed.
- How do we expand our definition of what's possible? In what ways have you been limited by a narrow definition of possibility?
- It was difficult for Joseph to fully embrace or understand this dream. It was a dream that depicted Joseph in a different position than was culturally expected. A major challenge might have been Joseph's unwillingness to see himself differently. How do you think God has called or is calling to you to embrace something different about yourself?

A Dream with No Details

- The book states, "An honest walk with God will lend you more questions than answers." What questions might this dream raise for Joseph?

- What questions has faith raised in your own life?
- Joseph is a seventeen-year-old kid searching for answers. He has a dream that he can't comprehend and is looking for someone to help him connect the dots. Describe an instance where you could not make sense of what God was doing in your life. Where did you go to search for answers? Whom did you trust?

Unpredictable

Invite a dreamer to read this passage aloud.

> God showed Joseph what appeared to be a place of prominence. The only problem was that there was no path that he could imagine that could take him from his current responsibilies to seeing his dream come to fruition. It's hard for him to truly embrace what he sees because there is no straight line from being out in the fields to having people bow at his feet. That gap between the dots is too great. The present and the picture of the future do not connect. . . . *Faith is not lived in straight lines.*

- What does that last phrase mean to you?
- Discuss the contradictions between Joseph's dreams and his present.
- Have there been instances where you felt the dots were not connecting in your own life? What emotions were attached to the disconnect?

They Can't See It

- Give a brief description of Joseph's dream from the viewpoint of his brothers. Encourage everyone to modernize the details and context.
- Next, give another description of Joseph's dream from the viewpoint of his father. Again, encourage the dreamers to modernize the details and context.
- People in close proximity won't always share the same beliefs. This can occur with family members,

spouses, friendships, coworkers, and so on. What are the benefits and difficulties of sharing these different perspectives?

- In what ways were the responses to Joseph's dreams something that stood in his way, preventing him from fulfilling them?
- In what ways did the responses to Joseph's dreams help to bring them about?

Love and Belief

- At this point in Joseph's life, everyone doubted the validity of his dream. How do you think Joseph interpreted their responses? How did they make him feel? Have you had experiences where someone doubted either your abilities or ideas, or both? What impact did that have on your willingness to dream or share future ideas?
- Replay the scenario. Upon hearing the details of Joseph's dream, how might his brothers or his father respond differently? Think of a response that acknowledges their doubt but still affirms Joseph in the process.
- What is the difference between love and belief? Which one do you desire? When do you need love? When do you need belief? Should people who love you always believe in you?

Closing the Session

Have a dreamer read this aloud:

> There are times when you might be the only one who believes. We must resist the urge to simply dream at a level that won't disappoint others or bring unwanted criticism. So, you will have to keep going back and forth to the fields, make the drive every day to the office, show up to the classroom, or keep the home in order while being the only

one who still sees the possibilities. This is not about trying to change the responses of others or even persuade the crowds that are the closest. It's not always about helping others see what they can't. Remember this was a dream not for his father, not for his brother, but it was given to Joseph. It is about how we respond to God's dream for our lives. Even when no one else can see it, will we believe it? Do you believe it? Do you still believe that God has a bigger picture for your life? Do you believe it, even if you can't fully see it at this moment?

Closing Prayer

End your session with the following prayer:

Merciful God, help us to see ourselves as dreamers. Not as people with great ideas, but those who want to see your will done in our lives and in our communities. Challenge us to see ourselves the way you see us. Peel away the limits we have placed on ourselves and on other people. Free us from our own minds. Stir in us new possibilities. Ignite our faith. Renew our passion. We open our faith and close our eyes so that we might see your bigger picture. In Jesus's name we pray. Amen.

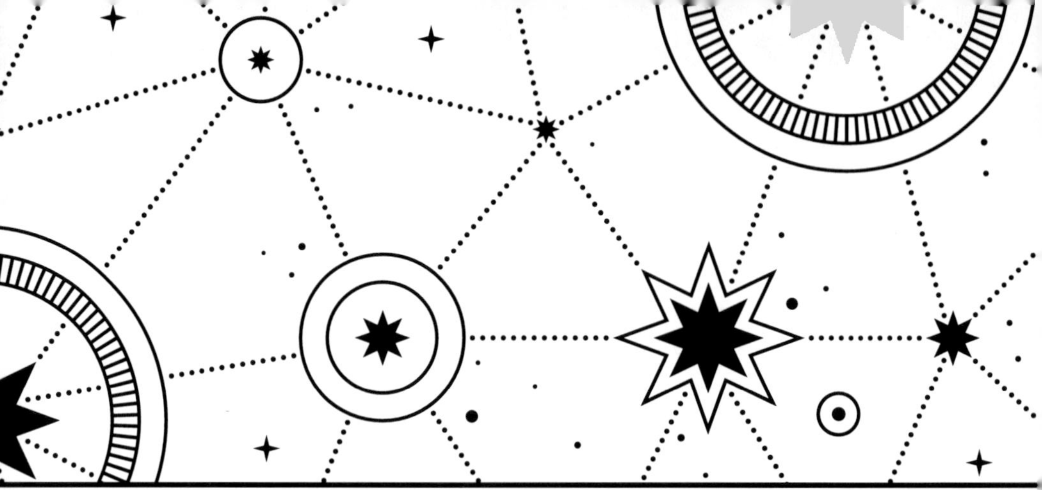

SESSION 2
I'M A SURVIVOR

Session Goals

In this session, dreamers will:

- examine the relationship between the dots they have survived and God's big picture for their lives,
- explore what survival meant for Joseph and what it means for today,
- learn not to overlook or discount these moments, but see God's presence even in the most challenging seasons along their faith journey,
- affirm that survival is a success, and
- examine ways that we hinder and obstruct the dream of others.

Biblical Foundation: *Genesis 37:19-24, 28*

The brothers said to each other, "Here comes the big dreamer. Come on now, let's kill him and throw him into one of the cisterns, and we'll say a wild animal devoured him. Then we will see what becomes of his dreams!"

When Reuben heard what they said, he saved him from them, telling them, "Let's not take his life." Reuben said to them, "Don't spill his blood! Throw him into this desert cistern, but don't lay a hand on him." He intended to save Joseph from them and take him back to his father.

When Joseph reached his brothers, they stripped off Joseph's long robe, took him, and threw him into the cistern, an empty cistern with no water in it. . . .

When some Midianite traders passed by, they pulled Joseph up out of the cistern. They sold him to the Ishmaelites for twenty pieces of silver, and they brought Joseph to Egypt.

Preparation

- Read chapter 2: "I'm a Survivor."
- Preview session 2 video.
- Set aside time to pray for the dreamers of your group. Say an intentional prayer for the difficulties and obstacles that each of them might be facing at this moment. Remember that each person in your group is or has gone through their own struggles and survived.
- Provide a few notebooks and pens to ensure that everyone can participate in the dream book activities.
- *Trigger Warning*: The session might surface painful thoughts that the dreamers have experienced. Resist the urge to "fix their situation." Use this time together to listen and invite God into that situation. The presence of the group speaks volumes.
- At the end of the session, there will be an invitation to ring a bell. While a small physical bell would be ideal, a prerecorded sound on your phone or even one found online will be sufficient.

Opening the Session

- Welcome everyone and thank them for returning. Invite those who attended session 1 to share any comments or insights that may have surfaced in the past week. Use this moment to recount the story of Joseph from all angles to give a complete picture of the narrative.
- Remind the dreamers of the nature of this session and the possibility of sensitive information arising. Invite those present to share only at the level of their comfort. Vulnerability looks different for each person.
- Remind the group that this is a safe space for sharing and encourage confidentiality.
- Ask the dreamers to refer to their dream books and open to the page filled with dots. Now invite them to draw and label more dots that represent the obstacles and difficulties that they have experienced.

Opening Prayer

Begin your session with the following prayer:

God, we invite you into this space—not just into this room, but into our hearts and into our lives. Remove anything that would hinder us from drawing closer during our time together. Free our minds and guide our conversation. We trust that in this moment you will stretch us, mold us, care for us, and love us. It is this love that not only meets us where we are but also doesn't leave us in the same condition. We are here today, not because of our own strength, but only because of your grace and mercy. In Jesus's name we pray. Amen.

Watch the Video

Play video for session 2 using your DVD player or stream with Amplify Media. Discuss the following:

- Invite the dreamers to share one to two main points that resonated with them from this session.

- What words would you use to describe Joseph's journey thus far?
- How would you define and describe modern-day pits?

Scripture and Book Study

Use the questions and activities below to discuss each section of the book and the Scripture passage for this chapter, Genesis 37:19-24, 28.

To See It, You Will Have to Survive It

Invite a dreamer to read this portion of the book aloud.

> It's tempting to start drawing the dream without connecting the obstacles. These are the dots we want to delete from the picture. They are the moments that we often pray would cease. We meticulously try to forge our image with as few of these moments as possible. And yet, without them, the picture is incomplete. Surviving is a part of every dreamer's experience. We pride ourselves on being dreamers. We celebrate the dreamers in our community. Undoubtedly, behind every dreamer is a survivor.

- What's your immediate response to this quote? Why do we so easily want to move beyond these difficult dots?
- Misplaced anger played a central role in this narrative. Joseph was merely a target for his brothers' anger. Their real issue was with their father. What's the danger when your feelings go unchecked or unresolved? How do you normally deal with difficult emotions?
- Impulsive decisions can affect the rest of our lives. What advice would you have given to either Joseph's brothers or his father, or both? How do we guard ourselves against impulsiveness?

Pits and Dark Places

- Given the descriptions provided for each kind of pit, take a moment to list a few examples under each category.

  - ◊ *Private pits*: the battles we fight behind closed doors
  - ◊ *Public pits*: the pits we want to hide, but we must live them out before public opinion.
  - ◊ *Systematic pits*: policies, practices, and procedures that continue to affect people's lives. Where do you find these in your community?
- Is there one category of pit that you are most familiar with?
- When have you found yourself in a pit or hard place? Where was it? How would you describe that experience? How did you get there?
- Think about the images of various pits, that is, difficult or painful circumstances, in our culture today. What attitudes do we often have regarding the kind of person who ends up in such places?
- How does the picture of Joseph in this position challenge our preconceived notions of pits?

Exit Doors

- Can you relate to Joseph's feelings of being trapped? Why or why not?
- Describe a past or recent incident where you felt as though there was no way out. Where did you look for the exit doors?
- What advice would you give to Joseph at this point in his journey?
- What lessons is Joseph learning through these experiences?

Nourished

- Verse 24 reminds the reader that there is no water in the cistern. That is the most compelling detail we get regarding Joseph's pit. What's the significance of this detail?
- You are nourished by more than just food and water. What gives you energy in this season of your life? What nourishes you? Where are those place where you are most nourished?

- What are the signs or indicators to know whether something is starving you or sustaining you?

Intervention

- What assumptions do you often make about where and how God will intervene in negative circumstances you face? How does Joseph's narrative deconstruct or support any of these assumptions?
- Discuss why it's so difficult for people to ask for help. What's the risk? What's at stake if we fail at asking for assistance?
- How would you rate your own readiness to ask for interventions?
  - ◊ 1 - Never
  - ◊ 2 - Sometimes
  - ◊ 3 - Often
  - ◊ 4 - Only when I'm extremely desperate!
- Share examples of when you have felt or seen God's intervention in your life or in a situation you've been close to. How do you think the outcome would have been different if God was not present?

Invite a dreamer to read this quote aloud:

> God wants to come into our lives. God doesn't just want to intervene through the dreams. God wants to intervene in the dark places where few want to visit. Are there areas of your life where you need God to intervene? Are there situations that are beyond your control, and you need help?

- Take a few moments to answer those questions among the group.

He Survived

Invite a dreamer to read this aloud:

> Perhaps Joseph is not at a place where he's seeking to understand the pit, because he is just trying to survive. It's

tempting to become reflective in similar situations. The assumption is that our understanding will yield a sense of endurance and strength waiting to be unleashed. We try to connect the dots to and from our pits.

At the moment, Joseph has no idea how and where this will end. He can't understand it. However, he can survive it. Joseph gives us a needed reminder that you can survive those moments when you do not understand. Comprehension is not a prerequisite for survival.

- What role does understanding often play in our attempt at survival?
- What does this suggest about God? What conclusions can you make about God with regard to the pits and hard places that you might be experiencing?
- There is often a stark difference in the ways that we celebrate "thriving" and "surviving." Take a moment to highlight these differences. As a culture, how can we change the narrative in a way that places a higher value on the act of survival?
- Make a list of the situations that Joseph has survived. What can you conclude about his personality and resolve?

We All Have a Role to Play

- While it is often easy to place ourselves in the role of Joseph, we have all been guilty of throwing others into a pit. How have you been guilty of creating unhealthy environments for others?
- Recall the names of those who have asked God for deliverance from you.
- Why do you think Joseph's brothers were able to continue with business as usual, knowing their brother was down in a pit? What does this suggest about our own lack of awareness?
- How was Joseph's survival a redeeming act for his brothers?

Fill In the Blank

- What are practical ways that you or your faith community can celebrate these dots of survival? Be specific.
- Let this be a reminder that you are a survivor. Take the prerogative to personalize the phrase "I am a survivor." Maybe you are a grief survivor, abuse survivor, church hurt survivor, divorce survivor, or low self-esteem survivor. The options are many; just fill in the blank. Regardless of how you describe it, let this be a part of your identity. Not because you are defined by it, but because it's a constant reminder of what you have been able to overcome with God's help. From the start of this journey of connecting the dots and seeing God's bigger picture, Joseph has reminded us that there isn't anything he can't overcome. When there was no way out, nothing to nourish him, God intervened and pulled him out. You have survived situations that you never imagined you would have to endure. To all the survivors, find a bell and ring it. Celebrate that you made it.
- Ask the dreamers to fill in the blank. I survived _______________. At the end of each response, ring the bell. For those who are not comfortable sharing verbally, invite them to simply write that phrase in their journal. When they have completed writing, be sure to ring the bell for them as well. Every dreamer should have a reminder that they, too, are survivors.

Closing the Session

Close the session by asking your fellow dreamers the following questions:

- What was helpful about today's session? What was challenging? Invite everyone to respond verbally and in their dream books.

Closing Prayer

End the session with the following prayer:

Merciful God, where would we be without you? As we move closer to seeing the bigger picture that you have for our lives, we know that it's not always easy. We acknowledge the difficulties. However, we also acknowledge your presence and your ability to meet us where we need you most. You are not just concerned with our dreams, you are also aware of our pits. You love us enough to meet us, heal us, and pull us out of places we thought were unredeemable. Forgive us for sometimes giving up too soon. Forgive us for being too proud to ask for help. Forgive us for the moments when we caused harm to others. Let us live each day as though we are people who have been rescued with and for a purpose. In Jesus's name we pray. Amen.

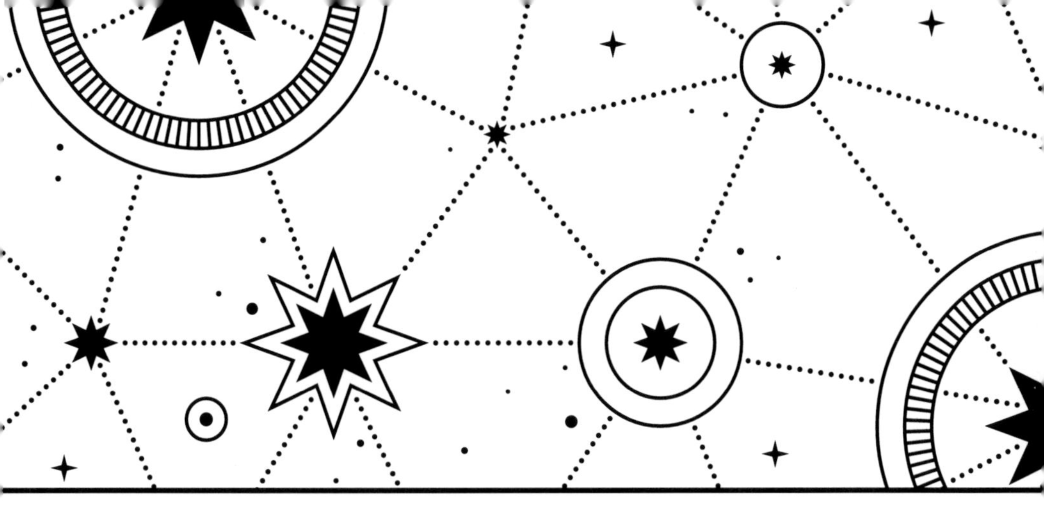

SESSION 3
DREAMING IN PRISON

Session Goals

In this session dreamers will consider the challenge of holding on to God's dream for their lives in adverse circumstances. It is one thing to have a dream; it's another to maintain it when life has led us to places of confinement, loss, and suffering. Here we will discover the invaluable spiritual lessons we learn from Joseph as he descends into a dungeon prison and what they mean for us today.

These lessons include:

- the relationship between our character, integrity, and maintaining God's dream for our life;
- a faith-filled response when dreams look dormant or dead;
- the unique role God gives other people in reengaging our spiritual memories and growing our faith in God's big picture for our lives; and

- why we can take risks in connecting to people around us despite the disappointment people have brought to our lives in the past.

Biblical Foundation: *Genesis 40:1-8*

Some time later, both the wine steward and the baker for Egypt's king offended their master, the king of Egypt. Pharaoh was angry with his two officers, the chief wine steward and the chief baker, and he put them under arrest with the commander of the royal guard in the same jail where Joseph was imprisoned. The commander of the royal guard assigned Joseph to assist them. After they had been under arrest for some time, both of them—the wine steward and the baker for Egypt's king who were imprisoned in the jail—had dreams one night, and each man's dream had its own meaning. When Joseph met them in the morning, he saw that they were upset. He asked the officers of Pharaoh who were under arrest with him in his master's house, "Why do you look so distressed today?"

They answered, "We've both had dreams, but there's no one to interpret them."

Joseph said to them, "Don't interpretations belong to God? Describe your dreams to me."

Preparation

- Read chapter 3, "Dreaming in Prison."
- Preview the session 3 video.
- Prepare your own heart through prayer or meditation to lead discussion on adversity and suffering.
- Set aside time to pray for the dreamers of your group prior to the session, as this discussion may trigger challenging memories or difficult current realities.
- Invite dreamers to bring potting soil, a small pot, and seeds to the session, or provide these materials to the group.

- Invite group members to bring their dream book journal with them to the session.

Opening the Session

- Issue a preface to the group that this may be a challenging conversation where past or present feelings of pain and suffering may be brought to the surface. Remind dreamers that through the presence of the Holy Spirit we can do hard things and have difficult conversations in love.
- Invite dreamers to gather their pots, soil, and seeds. Take a moment to plant the seeds in soil and water them. Ask the group to look at these pots and say whether these plants are living or dead.
- Invite them to consider that on the surface we can't tell either way, and that is how Joseph's life looked on the surface in today's Scripture. It may also be how our lives look to us during seasons of pain and challenge.
- Invite dreamers to consider a different perspective: underneath the surface, growth and God are present. We just may not be able to see it now.

Opening Prayer

Pray the following opening prayer or something similar:

Holy God, you are with us in the palaces and the prisons of our lives. Your spirit is ever present, even in places and with people that have brought pain and adversity. As we share our conversation today, be with us as we may touch on some of those tender parts of our own story through the narrative of Joseph. Help us to share with transparency but also to care for one another in love. May this session help us to see that you are always with us and leading us toward the big picture you have for our lives. Amen.

Watch the Video

Play video for session 2 using your DVD player or stream with Amplify Media. Discuss the following:

- What key ideas resonated with you in this video?
- What challenged you to think differently about God's dream for your life?
- Have you seen the difference between dormancy and death in your own spiritual life?

Scripture and Book Study

Use the questions and activities below to discuss each section of the book and the biblical passage for this chapter, Genesis 40:1-8.

Genesis 40:1-8

- Invite a dreamer to read these verses out loud
- Offer the following historical context: ancient Egypt did not have a network of systematized incarceration that we have today. Therefore, those accused of crimes were often held in makeshift prisons or dungeons like the one described in this Scripture.
- Without a system of standards and practices, accused prisoners could find themselves incarcerated for long stretches of time without any clarity as to when their incarceration would end.
- Additionally, there was no legal infrastructure that provided accused prisoners counsel or support. Prisoners like Joseph were entirely dependent upon someone advocating for them to Pharaoh or other high-ranking officials who could lead to their release.

Dreaming in a Nightmare

- Have there been seasons in your life when you have found it difficult to dream? What was happening in your life at the time?

- The experience of our global pandemic has exacerbated feelings of isolation, depression, and disconnection. How did the global pandemic influence your ability to dream?
- Nicole describes feeling as if she is living in a nightmare as she walks alongside people's experiences with adversity and suffering. Where have you had to walk alongside someone's nightmare? What did you invite them to dream again?

Conditions and Character

- Joseph finds himself in a dungeon. When in your life have you felt spiritually or emotionally imprisoned?
- What did that experience do to the dream or vision you and God had for your life?
- External conditions have the power to influence our internal condition. How does Joseph respond to being in prison? Does it alter his character or integrity? How do you think you would respond underneath such constraints?
- Invite dreamers to consider who they are in Christ. Ask them to identify additional Scriptures that call us to maintain our character in Christ in the midst of external conditions that challenge it. Such Scriptures may include:
    - ◊ *Romans 12:2*: Don't be conformed to the patterns of this world, but be transformed by the renewing of your minds so that you can figure out what God's will is—what is good and pleasing and mature.
    - ◊ *John 15:19*: If you belonged to the world, the world would love you as its own. However, I have chosen you out of the world, and you don't belong to the world. This is why the world hates you.

Looking Beneath the Surface

- What dreams are dormant in your life today?
- How might God be preparing you underneath the surface in this season?

- Seeing that our dreams are dormant and not dead may take some convincing. Invite participants to name a spiritual practice they will use to remind themselves that God is still at work. They may consider writing dream affirmations on Post-It Notes in places where they are often present, such as the car, bathroom mirror, or refrigerator door.
- When you return for the following session, ask people if seeing these affirmations regularly made an impact on how they saw themselves and their character in Christ.

Faith for the In-Between

Invite a dreamer to read this passage aloud:

> What you do until then is a daily arching of the neck, a deliberate adjustment of the gaze that sometimes still hurts, but every day, a little less.
>
> Until the dream comes into view, we make a daily faith choice to look up with expectation.

- Invite the group to react to this passage. How would they respond to this question, What do I do until then? What faith strategies do they use in the space between having the dream and living the dream?
- Are there spiritual strengths or blessings we gain while our dreams are dormant that we would forfeit if we never experienced this season of waiting?
- Consider other biblical characters, like Abraham and Sarah, who received a dream but struggled to see it until it became a reality. What do we learn from their experience?
- This section ends with the invitation to look up. What have you been focused on during seasons of dormancy and how is God inviting you to take a wider view today?

Tell Me Your Dreams

- Are you a part of the 99.9% who find it difficult to dream while your dreams are stalled? Why are those experiences so painful?
- Hearing the dreams of others requires a shift from a scarcity to an abundant mindset. Invite dreamers to consider God's promises of abundance throughout Scripture. Some of these may include the following:
    - ◊ *2 Corinthians 9:8*: God has the power to provide you with more than enough of every kind of grace. That way, you will have everything you need always and in everything to provide more than enough for every kind of good work.
    - ◊ *Philippians 4:19*: My God will meet your every need out of his riches in the glory that is found in Christ Jesus.
    - ◊ *John 10:10*: The thief enters only to steal, kill, and destroy. I came so that they could have life—indeed, so that they could live life to the fullest.
- Our spiritual memories can have difficulty recalling God's faithfulness as we live through extended seasons of dormancy. When did someone or something jog your spiritual memory?
- Invite dreamers to help stir up one another's spiritual memories and share a time when God refreshed their faith in the midst of waiting.

Lost and Found

This section makes the theological claim that "sometimes the dot you need to connect God's big picture for your life is in someone else's dream."

- Who are people in your life who have been dream coproducers? Are they family members, friends, acquaintances, or even strangers?

- Past hurts and betrayals can make it difficult to risk collaborating with people on God's dreams for our lives. How have you been hurt by others? Does that hurt influence your willingness to connect with others today?
- Whom might God be calling you to forgive in this season so that you are set free to dream again?
- Answer the central chapter question as a group:
    - ◊ Whom has God placed in your life to coproduce your dream?
    - ◊ Share responses as a group or create time to reflect on this in dream book journals.

Closing the Session

This chapter ends with the thought: "when the unknown goodness of people meets with the certain goodness of God, I can take a risk."

- Close the session by acknowledging the risk dreamers are taking in this journey of study together. Invite dreamers to close their time together by practicing a Connect the Dream affirmation circle.
- Invite the group of dreamers to form a circle. One at a time, each dreamer should stand in the center of the circle.
- Dreamers around the circle can take turns writing or saying out loud affirmations about the dreamer inside the circle. *For example*: "Dreamer, you have survived unspeakable pain and heartache. Yet, I can see God using you to heal others. Keep dreaming."
- Continue the exercise until each dreamer has had a chance to stand in the center of the circle.

Closing Prayer

At the end of this exercise offer a closing prayer:

"God of our dormant years and God of our fruitful seasons, we thank you that you are Immanuel: a God who is always with us. We pray now

for each dreamer that you have connected us to through the study. Remind us throughout this week that you are sure when others are not. You are someone we can trust when we fail one another. Help us to see the coproducers of dreams in our midst and to be willing to collaborate with others on the big picture you have for their lives. God, we are so grateful that you have been constantly at work underneath the surface, and we surrender ourselves to you knowing that in due season we will reap a great harvest."

- Invite dreamers to nurture their plants over the next several weeks and to let them be a living illustration of how God nurtures our dreams underneath the surface.

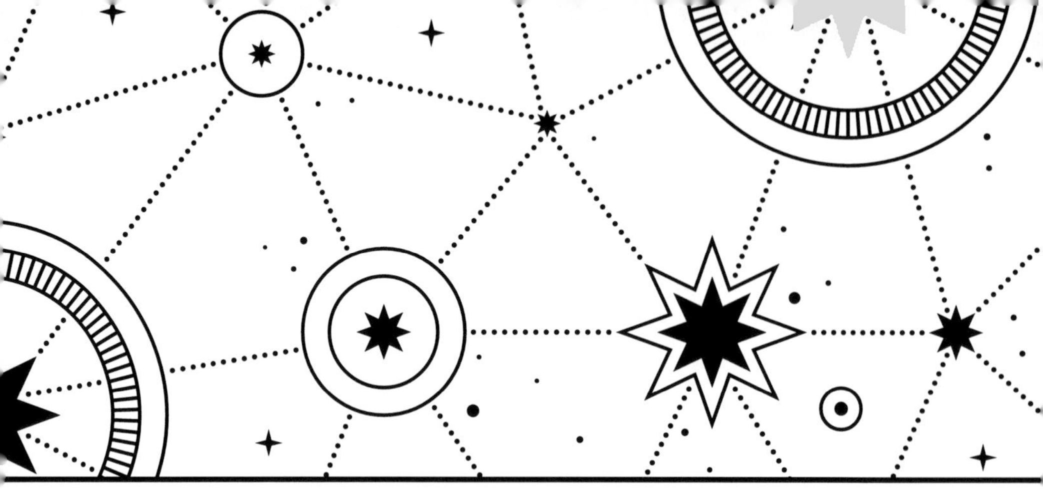

CHAPTER 4
TIMING IS EVERYTHING

Session Goals

In this session dreamers will:

- understand the relationship between timing and God's big picture for our lives;
- analyze Joseph's narrative through these selected Scripture verses and recognize how God's timing becomes clear;
- consider the ways in which God has orchestrated events and relationships in their lives that lead to God's big picture;
- explore the ways in which God has connected the dots of their big picture, including the people, places, and faith lessons learned along the way; and
- begin to see no season of their lives has been wasted.

Biblical Foundation: *Genesis 41:1, 8-16*

Two years later, Pharaoh dreamed that he was standing near the Nile. . . . In the morning, he was disturbed and summoned all of Egypt's religious experts and all of its advisors. Pharaoh described his dreams to them, but they couldn't interpret them for Pharaoh.

Then the chief wine steward spoke to Pharaoh: "Today I've just remembered my mistake. Pharaoh was angry with his servants and put me and the chief baker under arrest with the commander of the royal guard. We both dreamed one night, he and I, and each of our dreams had its own interpretation. A young Hebrew man, a servant of the commander of the royal guard, was with us. We described our dreams to him, and he interpreted our dreams for us, giving us an interpretation for each dream. . . .

So Pharaoh summoned Joseph, and they quickly brought him from the dungeon. He shaved, changed clothes, and appeared before Pharaoh. Pharaoh said to Joseph, "I had a dream, but no one could interpret it. Then I heard that when you hear a dream, you can interpret it."

Joseph answered Pharaoh, "It's not me. God will give Pharaoh a favorable response."

Preparation

- Prepare your spirit for this session by bringing a physical copy of your calendar for the week to the session. Consider every meeting and every planned event. Invite dreamers to bring a copy of their calendars for the week as well. You will utilize these calendars as a tool to demonstrate our surrendering to God's timing. (*Note*: This should be a copy only, printed or photocopies. The calendars will be destroyed in the activity, so don't bring the actual calendar you use for planning things!)

- Additionally, bring paper and writing utensils for dreamers to chart the dots God has been connecting in their own lives.
- Prior to the session, make a chart connecting the dots in God's big picture for your life. Within the session, you will use it as a model to demonstrate to the dreamers what this may look like (see p. 51 of this leader guide).

Opening the Session

- Invite dreamers to bring copies of their calendars for the week. This calendar will be utilized for the closing activity of the session.
- Welcome participants as they arrive and thank them for returning. Invite each person to share something significant they have learned over the past three weeks as a result of this study.
- Share with the dreamers that this session is an invitation, through the narrative of Joseph's life, to surrender our time to God.

Opening Prayer

Open with this prayer:

"God, you say in your Word that there is a season for everything. But your divine timing governs everything in creation. We pray now that this divine timing would also govern our hearts and faith. As we study the story of Joseph's life, we pray that you would stir up a desire within us to turn our lives and our time over to you. We trust, O God, that your timing is everything and that your plan is the big picture for our lives. Be with us now as we dream, learn, and discern together. Amen."

Watch the Video

Play the video for session 4 on your DVD player, or stream via Amplify Media. Discuss the following questions:

- Are there instances in your life where you experienced the difference the right timing makes?
- What challenges you about God's timing and the plans you may have for your own life?
- What might we miss without God's divine timing?

Scripture and Book Study

Use the questions and activities below to discuss each section of the book and the biblical passage for this chapter, Genesis 41:1-16.

Genesis 41:1-16

- Read the Scripture aloud and offer the following historical perspective:
  - ◊ Egyptian religious culture was polytheistic. Believers ascribed to several anthropomorphic images of gods and believed that divine beings often communicated through dreams.
  - ◊ Pharaohs would have multiple magicians or wise men who would offer prophecies and dream interpretation.
  - ◊ A foreign prisoner of a different religious background offering dream interpretation would have been a cultural and religious exception in the court of Pharaoh. Yet, God's timing creates a watershed moment where Joseph's gifts, Pharaoh's needs, and the cupbearer's memory align.

Go/No-Go

Prior to the session or within the session invite dreamers to watch this clip from the feature film *Hidden Figures*: https://youtu.be/JAEnv1PvBvw.

Ask dreamers to consider the following questions:

- Do you understand the equation that's being written on the board?

- How might this clip reflect the complex timing God orchestrates in the big picture of each of our lives?
- Do you recognize the difference between believing God will do something and surrendering to when God will do it?
- Invite dreamers to share Scriptures that remind us that waiting on God's timing is a part of the journey of discipleship. Scriptures might include:
  - ◊ *Psalm 130:5*: I hope, LORD. My whole being hopes, and I wait for God's promise.
  - ◊ *Habakkuk 2:3*: There is still a vision for the appointed time; it testifies to the end; it does not deceive. If it delays, wait for it; for it is surely coming; it will not be late.
  - ◊ *Isaiah 40:31*: But those who hope in the LORD will renew their strength; they will fly up on wings like eagles; they will run and not be tired; they will walk and not be weary.
- What are the two ways in which we often interpret waiting?
- How is waiting on God different?
- Share a time when you later understood that waiting on God was an act of grace.

Grace, Timing, and Place

This section includes the passage: "The reason why the years aren't wasted is not simply because of what God is doing around us, but the gift God is developing privately within us."

- What gifts has God been developing in you privately?
- How might God one day use those gifts publicly?
- Walk the dreamers through each dot on Joseph's time line in this section. Do they see the connections God was making? What connection might God be making in their lives?

- Offer to the group the opportunity to connect the dots of God's big picture for their lives from the past to present. Give each dreamer paper and pencil. Invite them to consult the dots in their dream book representing dreams and difficult experiences, then rearrange these dots in a timeline of opportunities, people, and gifts that connected over time. Invite them to describe or draw what happened at each dot. Invite dreamers to share their connect-the-dots dream map with the larger group. What patterns do they see? What was unexpected? What was likely?

How Did I Get Here?

Invite dreamers to consult their connect-the-dots dream map again. In this section of the chapter we acknowledge that the past can also bless us. Ask dreamers to identify the dots in their past that showed up as blessings in their future. Discuss the following questions:

- What dots would not have connected if you had not treated people well?
- What dots or people from your past matter in your life today?
- Who in your life needs to be reminded that they matter, or that they played a significant role in connecting God's big picture for your life?
- Invite the dreamers to express gratitude to those people who were coproducers of God's dream.

Timing and Testimony

Reflect on this insight from this section: "God's dream for your life is never just that you use your gifts, but that you grow in your faith."

- How has Joseph's faith grown since we first met him?
- What evidence of this do we see in Scripture?

- What was Joseph's personality like in the past? How did this influence the way he shared his dream or interacted with others? What do these verses reveal about Joseph's approach now?
- To whom does Joseph point the dreamer when he offers an interpretation? What does this shift indicate about his faith today as opposed to when we first met him?
- Invite dreamers to look at their connect-the-dots picture again. This time invite them to identify how God grew their faith at each dot.
- What did God teach them in that place or through that relationship?
- How did God use what they learned on one dot to connect to the dot where God was taking them next?
- God grows our faith and testimony over time. What other biblical characters are an example of this?
- Offer the life of David as an example of this truth.
    - ◊ Share with the group that approximately seventeen years passed between David's anointing as king and his ascension into the role.
    - ◊ How did God grow David's faith while he waited for the timing to align with God's big picture that he become king of Israel?
- Ask dreamers to share and identify other biblical characters whose lives demonstrate this.

You're Ready

We spend years trying to connect the dots to God's big picture for our lives. Yet when all of God's timing lines up and we finally take the first step into our destiny it can be terrifying.

- What do you think was going through Joseph's mind as he walked through Pharaoh's palace? Do you think he felt completely confident? Do you think he may have felt pangs of fear or uncertainty?

- Invite dreamers to look at their connect-the-dots map again.
- As they trace their steps from dot to dot, did they always feel completely confident?
- Did they ever experience fear or self-doubt?
- What helped them move from dot to dot in spite of their fear?
- How might God use our fear to create trust?

Closing the Session

Invite the dreamers to get the physical copy of their weekly calendar. Each dreamer should pass the calendar to the person sitting next to him or her. Instruct each person to tear those physical copies to shreds. This is a dramatic act, but it is an opportunity to reflect on the following:

- How does it feel to give your calendar to someone else?
- Were you anxious, relieved, or in shock when your calendar was ripped to shreds?
- What faith lesson may we learn in ripping up our own time lines?
- What would it look like to make schedules to manage our lives but to also surrender those plans to God's final revisioning?
- Before you move into the closing of the session, invite dreamers to share their connect-the-dots map with someone they are close to who is not present. Perhaps even someone who is a part of one of those dots. This could be an invitation for others to dream alongside them or to begin the process of seeing God's big picture for their lives.
- In this session invite dreamers to pray with one another and then close the group with corporate prayer. Invite

dreamers to ask one another to finish the following sentences:

◊ Today I see how God connected the dots to___________.

◊ Today I see how God connected me to this person who _________.

◊ Today I ask for prayer as _____________.

Closing Prayer

End your session with the following prayer:

"Holy God, if we had ten thousand tongues it would not be enough to express our gratitude to you. For as we take inventory of our lives, we cannot help seeing the ways in which you have moved. You put us in the right places, with the right people, and at the right time so that your big picture for our lives could continue to emerge. God, forgive us when we have moved by our time line and not yours. Forgive us when we failed to treat people you placed in our lives with worthiness and respect. Help us now, O God, to move by faith and not by fear. We know that you are preparing us each and every day for your dream for our lives. May we continue to see that your timing is everything. In Jesus's name we pray. Amen."

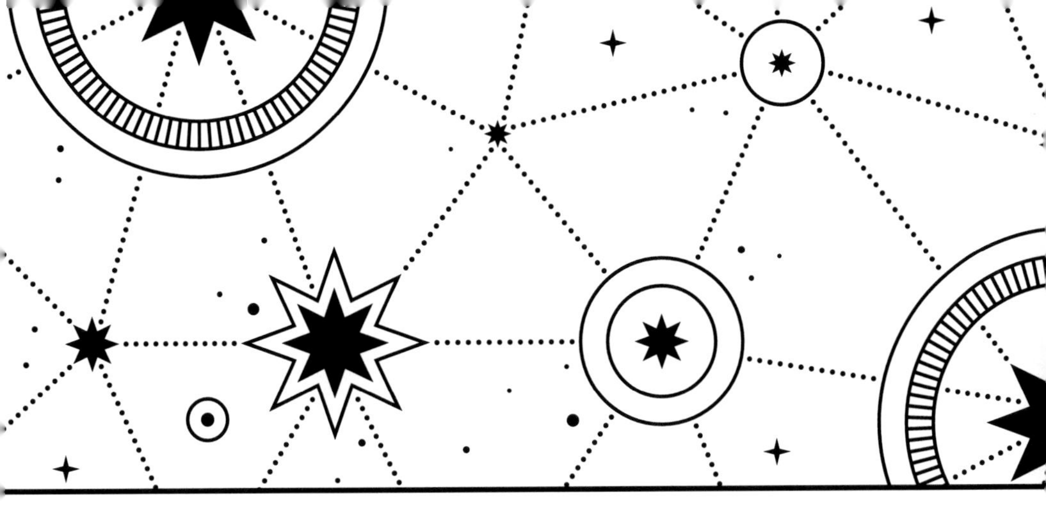

CHAPTER 5

THE MOMENT WE'VE BEEN WAITING FOR

Session Goals

In this session, dreamers will:

- finally see the big picture of God's dream for Joseph's life,
- assess where they are in their own dreams and consider the relationship between starting points and God's outcomes,
- discover and reflect on Joseph's familial trauma and how these unhealed wounds show up in God's big picture for his life and their own, and
- be equipped with critical questions to discern whether a dream's source is from God or oneself.

Biblical Foundations: *Genesis 45:1-8*

Joseph could no longer control himself in front of all his attendants, so he declared, "Everyone, leave now!" So no one stayed with him when he revealed his identity to his brothers. He wept so loudly that the Egyptians and Pharaoh's household heard him. Joseph said to his brothers, "I'm Joseph! Is my father really still alive?" His brothers couldn't respond because they were terrified before him.

Joseph said to his brothers, "Come closer to me," and they moved closer. He said, "I'm your brother Joseph! The one you sold to Egypt. Now, don't be upset and don't be angry with yourselves that you sold me here. Actually, God sent me before you to save lives. We've already had two years of famine in the land, and there are five years left without planting or harvesting. God sent me before you to make sure you'd survive and to rescue your lives in this amazing way. You didn't send me here; it was God who made me a father to Pharaoh, master of his entire household, and ruler of the whole land of Egypt.

Preparation

- Prepare your own spirit for this session by praying for each dreamer in your group. Ask God to continue to stir up the dream for their lives and your own.
- Remind each dreamer to bring their dream book journal to the session.
- Bring enough stationery cards, envelopes, and writing utensils for each dreamer in your group. You will utilize these for the closing activity of the session.

Opening the Session

- Open the session by expressing gratitude to each dreamer for the journey you've been on together.

- Invite dreamers as they are comfortable to share a phrase, statement, or learning from the first entry in their dream book journal. Then ask them to share a piece from their latest entry. Discuss the differences in their sentiments from the first session and today. What has changed or shifted over time?
- Share with the group that today's session includes a spiritual practice called healing memories. This may trigger painful memories from their past, and people should participate or share as they feel comfortable.

Opening Prayer

Open with the following prayer:

God, thank you for bringing us on this journey of study and faith together. We see the ways in which you have grown our faith and our relationships with one another. May your spirit of healing and wholeness be here in the midst of our final session today as we continue to seek your big picture for each of our lives. Amen.

Watch the Video

Play the video for session 5 on the DVD or stream via Amplify Media. Discuss the following questions:

- In this session we stand with Joseph at the moment he's been waiting for. Where can you specifically point to dots where God answered prayers in your life?
- After watching this session's video, how do you look at your dreams differently?
- What's your greatest takeaway from this series?

Scripture and Book Study

Invite one of the dreamers to read the Scripture passage, Genesis 45:1-8, out loud. Use the questions below to discuss each section of the book as well as the Scripture passage.

Started from the Bottom, Now We're Here

- Invite dreamers to name the narratives of the following biblical origin and outcomes:
  - ◊ began as a shepherd and became a king (David)
  - ◊ began as a fugitive murderer and became a liberator of his people (Moses)
  - ◊ began as a foreign widow and became a married ancestor of Jesus (Ruth)
  - ◊ began as a tax collector and became a disciples of Jesus (Matthew)
  - ◊ began as an unmarried pregnant teenager and became the mother of the Messiah (Mary)
- What do we learn about our origins and God's ability to connect the dots to our big picture?
- Does where we start determine where we end up with God?

Is This the Moment?

Throughout the book, we've considered the phrase, "life is lived forward but understood backward." Revisit your connect-the-dots dream time line in your journal and discuss the following:

- What does this phrase mean to you?
- How is this idea illustrated in these Scripture verses of Joseph's life and your own?
- What experiences have you already lived but are just now coming to understand the meaning of?

Success Doesn't Heal All Wounds

Read the Scripture passage for today aloud again. Invite the group to listen for every word or action describing Joseph's emotional state.

- After you have finished reading, invite the dreamers to name the words and actions they heard. These words will include:

- ◊ no longer control
- ◊ cried out
- ◊ wept
- ◊ loudly

- Are these words that have been associated with Joseph before?
- What do we learn about Joseph's unhealed trauma from these verses?
- Has unhealed pain and family trauma ever shown up in your life?
- How did it affect you? What impact did it have physically, spiritually, and emotionally?

Invite a dreamer to read this this passage aloud:

> Joseph reveals to us that success and even fulfilled dreams do not heal old wounds. We can't outrun every uncomfortable dot. We can't try to bury them under the accomplishments of others. The effects and impacts of certain dots linger beneath the surface of success. Something triggers those memories, and we realize that certain dots still impact us. It's hard to embrace the idea that elevation doesn't heal emotions. The dreams coming true won't solve all of our problems. It does not eliminate every struggle. It does not erase the hurt.

- How does that passage resonate with your experience?
- Has success erased old wounds? Why or why not?
- What unhealed hurts might lie beneath the surface in your life, waiting to be dealt with?
- Joseph's reaction to seeing his brothers was audible to the entire court.
- Have you created space in your life to heal? Where and who might that space include and exclude? Where might God be calling you to take refuge and heal today?

Now I See It

When we wrote the sentence, "God is not obligated to help us fulfill our dreams," it hurt just to type it! This idea goes against everything we have been socialized to believe about our own dreams and God's desires to fulfill them. Yet, Joseph's life challenges us to consider and embrace the uncomfortable truth that there may be a difference between our dreams and God's dream for our lives.

This requires us to deeply discern the source of our dreams. Invite dreamers to reflect on the following questions through journaling:

- What dream do you believe God has for your life?
- Is God a central figure in that dream? Will achieving the dream require your trust and dependence on God?
- Does the dream require you to compromise who you are? Does it stretch you but also affirm your God-given uniqueness?
- Does the dream reach beyond you? Will it serve and bless other people?
- After taking a few minutes for dreamers to respond in their journals, invite the group to share responses as they feel led.

Saying Goodbye

- Dreamers have taken the time to consider the source of their dreams. In that previous exercise, they may have noticed a gap between God's big expansive dream for their lives and their own desires. This section calls us to say goodbye. To let go of the picture we may have held for our lives and to embrace God's bigger picture.

This is not easy but in truth, we have to let go of our dreams for our lives before we can embrace God's big picture.

- **Ask dreamers:** What did you want to be when you grew up at age three, ten, or twenty-one? Were each of those responses the same? Or did they shift? Would it be possible to pursue all of these dreams at once?

This section challenges us with this truth: "we arrive at a critical point where it's clear that in order to see God's bigger picture, we must say goodbye to our dreams. It hurts. It feels like the death of a family member."

- What dreams might God be calling you to say goodbye to so that you can embrace God's Big Picture for your life?
- Who do you need to say no to in order to say yes to God? Is one of those people yourself?

Reframing: What Are You Bringing to the Moment

In this section of the book, we introduce the practice of healing memories.

- This practice begins by inviting dreamers to close their eyes, put their feet flat on the floor, and place their hands gently in their laps.
- You may ask them to turn their palms upright.
- Once everyone is in this position, invite dreamers into a time of intentional breathing. Intentional breathing includes long, deep inhales of cool air through the nose and long, deep exhales of warm air through the nose.
- Instruct the group to notice their breathing and to slowly relax each muscle in their bodies as they melt into their seats.
- Do this for at least three minutes, or until there is a sense of calm and relaxation in the room.
- Now, you are ready to move from breathing to memory. With eyes still closed, ask the group to remember a painful childhood memory. Ask them to consider:
    - ◊ Where were you?
    - ◊ What was done?
    - ◊ What was said?
    - ◊ Who else is in that memory?
    - ◊ What faces do you see?
    - ◊ How does it make you feel?
- Invite them to stay in that place for the next several minutes.

- Remind them to breathe. It is possible that, like Joseph, some may have an audibly emotional response to these past traumas. Assure people to breathe and of your presence.
- Now, we turn to the central aim of this exercise. Tell dreamers to imagine that Jesus has now entered that space of pain. Jesus is standing right next to them. Ask them what would Jesus say to them in that moment?
- Invite them to continue their breathing and linger in that space for several minutes.
- After a few moments have passed, instruct the dreamers to open their eyes and invite those who are willing to share or describe their experiences.
- Those who may not want to share may be invited to write in their dream book journals and reflect on their experiences later. Share with the group that the goal is not to change the past but, as we see in the life of Joseph, to reframe it.
- How did Joseph reframe his family trauma in these verses?
- How does the dynamic shift when we invite Jesus into our most painful childhood memories?
- Are there places in your life where God may be inviting you to reframe the way you saw yourself, others, and Jesus?

Credit

You've reached the final section of the book and the study series. This would be a great time to thank dreamers for being on this journey with you. An important idea to share is that Joseph's reframing of his trauma gave him the perspective that God's dots were connecting to a bigger picture. The picture that God envisioned was one where Joseph was in a place of power in order to serve other people, including his family.

Invite dreamers to reflect on this closing question:

- How are the dots that God is connecting in your life helping to serve other people?
- After people have had an opportunity to share, pass out the stationery and envelopes you gathered before the beginning of the session. Invite each dreamer to write a note of encouragement to another dreamer in the room. You will collect each of these notes and during the first full week after the session you can mail them to each dreamer. These notes will serve as reminders of what has been gleaned from these sessions and encourage people to keep living into God's big, expansive dream for their lives.

Closing Prayer

As you close, offer the dreamers the opportunity to say The Dreamer's Prayer together:

God, I want your dream for my life.
Nothing smaller.
Nothing limited.
Nothing inherited.
Nothing compared.
Nothing muted.
Your big, expansive dream.
Impossible for me to see without you.
Impossible for me to do without you.
Impossible for me to be without you.
Let me dream.
Let me dream.
Let me dream, again.

Made in United States
North Haven, CT
29 May 2024

53090113R10037